GUARD

YOUR

GATES

SIMPLE STEPS TO HIGH PRODUCTIVITY

ROD PATTERSON

ROD PATTERSON

No part of this publication may be reproduced, stored in a retrieval system or transmitted in any way by any means, electronic, mechanical, photocopy, recording or otherwise without the prior permission of the author except as provided by USA copyright law.

Author Photo: Brian Everett Francis (Phazion)

ROD PATTERSON

GUARD YOUR GATES

ROD PATTERSON

DEDICATION

To Katrina, my love and my hero.

ROD PATTERSON

ACKNOWLEDGMENTS

Being known as Katrina's husband and Ericka and Shane's father is one of my greatest joys in life. Whether I am victorious or defeated when I face the giants of the world, I always return home to a hero's welcome. You are my gift from God, and I am forever thankful. You inspire my vision.

My vision is to know God and to live life in appreciation of His grace. It is to be an irresistible husband to my wife and a loving father to my children as I model manhood in Christ and pursue success in my vocation.

Thank God for allowing me to be influenced by great leaders such as, Rev. A. R. Bernard, my Pastor; Dr. Onorio Chaparro, my friend and brother; my family, especially my wife and children.

Also, "thank you" to my father, Jerry; my incredible mom, whom I miss daily; my big sister, Leslie; my late, classy brother Darryl, my brother Jerry, Jr. and my big brother Hal for helping to shape me into the man God called me to be. I also acknowledge My International Christian Brotherhood Brothers and my Elsmere Family from the Bronx, NY.

CONTENTS

ROD PATTERSON

Welcome!

Thank you for picking up this book. I hope that as you read it, you will find information inside that will help you achieve excellence in all aspects of your life. The lessons that I share are transferrable. So while I have focused on business initiatives here, this book can help you in your personal life as well. I wrote this book because, at times, I have been a victim of not following the lessons shared but I have also been a beneficiary. I am a personal witness to their effectiveness and now live by these lessons.

We live in an information age. At a time

where the world is continually going paperless, information is exploding. How do you manage all of the information thrown at you? Guard Your Gates is a collection of quick lessons that will help you do the following:

1.   ORGANIZE YOUR GATES,

2.   DEFEND YOUR GATES, and

3.   GUARD YOUR GATES

In this age of information, many of us are finding it ever increasingly difficult to manage all of the information coming at us from many mediums. Whether through your email gate, desk gate, or mobile phone gate, you can become overwhelmed by an avalanche of incoming data and potentially

miss key communications that require your

attention.

This book contains my answer for all of

those challenges. It is written for professionals

looking for an edge in a competitive corporate

environment. This book can work well for Non-

Profits and Businesses alike as a supplement to their

onboarding program for new hires. Students who

are managing multiple classes and projects will find

this system can help them meet deadlines and stay

on track.

If you have ever been overwhelmed by a

seemingly insurmountable workload, and deadlines,

then this book is for you. If you want to be known

for being on top of your game, then this book will

help you get there. However, if you have ever been

reprimanded at work because you did not

acknowledge important, time sensitive

correspondence, then this book is definitely for you!

PREFACE

I got into the company car and left the parking lot of the company I worked at for a decade. I had just agreed to accept a severance package and walk away, ending my career there. It was a dark moment for me. Feeling defeated, worn, and stressed, I entered the highway and headed home. However, the farther away I drove from the building, the freer I felt. With each mile I passed, a ton of bricks fell off my back, but it was not supposed to be like this. This was the company where I expected to retire. As I listened to the wheels of the company's Chevy Impala roll down the highway, I reflected on my rise at the company as well as my ultimate fall. What happened?

"My Gates Were Overrun"

At work, there was a time when I had a good reputation for providing excellent customer service. My manager was pleased with my performance and my workload was very manageable. Then, out of nowhere, I got hit with a crisis. My mother was diagnosed with cancer. I did not realize the impact that her diagnosis had on me at the time, but later, as I looked back, I realized that it had a tremendous effect on me, personally and professionally.

I had been taking mom for her chemo and radiation treatments while commuting daily from Long Island to Westchester and back to Long Island every day. I would leave early in the morning, pick up mom in the Bronx to take her to receive chemo treatments and then back home. Then, off to work in Westchester and then back to Long Island, but not before heading back to the Bronx to check on mom. It was brutal. I had many family and work responsibilities to manage, and I was also heavily involved in men's ministry at my church. While I believed I had everything under control, I did not realize how my performance was slipping, causing my work product to suffer. As the months passed, my gates began to become overrun.

When my manager pointed this out, I then shared with him my mom's diagnosis. I explained all of the additional responsibilities I had taken on to assist in her care and get her the treatment she needed. My siblings and I were working together to help mom recover. I was doing my best to manage it all. Yet, several weeks later, I found myself reading, because this time it was in writing, an email from my manager letting me know that my performance was not up to par. To say that I was disappointed is an understatement. It seemed like the harder I tried, the farther back I fell. My manager pointed out that I was not measuring up.

I took exception to this because I had received many acknowledgements, accolades, and awards from senior management within this organization for going above and beyond the call of duty to now being told I am not even measuring up. This harsh reality of some companies in corporate America that I was now experiencing is captured in the name of a song sung by Janet Jackson: *"What Have You Done for Me Lately?"*

After multiple emails and meetings with my manager concerning my performance and still taking care of my mom, it finally came to a head when Human Resources called me in for a meeting. While I expected to be reprimanded for "not measuring up", the HR Manager told me that it was obvious that my mother's sickness was having an effect on my work product, and as a result, he would give me a paid week off to regain balance. I was so shocked by his generosity that I broke down and cried right there in his office.

Soon after I returned to work, mom passed away. Not long after that, the company began forcing me out. They eventually offered me a severance package, and since I did not have the mind, will, nor the energy to contest it, I accepted the package and decided to move on after a ten year run at this organization. Even though I decided to move on, I left bitter and disillusioned. Was the paid week off based on genuine compassion for me, my mom, and my situation or was it to placate me into thinking they had my best interest at heart? So

I left in disgrace to face an uncertain future. After

leaving, I took some time to refresh and reflect and

came to the conclusion that I made myself

vulnerable by not guarding my gates. There's no

question that the situation with my mom, her illness,

and her passing were devastating, and because it

was devastating, it lured me away from my gates.

But, could this have been avoided?

"I was determined to succeed"

It was not until I had an opportunity to

refresh and reflect that I realized that all of my gates

had become overrun. My email gate, mobile phone

gate, and all of my other gates were all overrun.

After taking an honest and hard look at myself, I realized that I couldn't really fault the company. While I had many talents and had received many accolades, I couldn't escape the truth which was that I had left many of my gates unguarded.

After a three month break, I was offered a position with another company. Even though I was still grieving mom's passing and still upset about the treatment I received at my prior company, I was determined to succeed. And succeed I did! I began to organize, defend, and guard my gates, and after a few years, I had developed a reputation at work and in my private life as one who is on top of everything.

That reputation has helped me to continually increase my value and helped me re-establish a personal brand that produces excellent results. In this book, I will share how I got there, and hopefully, you will benefit from lessons that were birthed out of my challenges. *Guard Your Gates!*

ROD PATTERSON

INTRODUCTION

"Why a gate in the first place?"

At my home, I have a gate around the perimeter of my property. The purpose of the gate is to create boundaries and provide some privacy. I remember getting frustrated because an unknown person in my neighborhood refused to curb their dog. Before we installed the gate, I used to find dog poop on my grass. And this was no small dog! I found it one time too many so I purchased and installed a gate to enclose our entire lawn. After that, I only found dog poop on the perimeter of my property and not on my lawn. The gate was both practical and symbolic: on the one hand, it kept the unknown dog walker at a distance, and on the other

27

hand, it also said, "I know you're here." But, why is that important? It is important because people like to do the wrong thing in anonymity. A dog walker will gladly let their dog excrete on your lawn while you are sleeping. However, on a bright sunny day while you are sitting on the porch, they will walk their dog somewhere else or, at the very least, they will curb it.

"Why is my gate open?"

Every now and then, after I mow the lawn, I, unknowingly don't always close the gate all the way. So the next day, when I pull into the driveway and see the gate open, I get concerned and wonder,

"Why is my gate open?"

As the gatekeeper of my home, it is my responsibility to ensure that our home is secure. With the gate left open, I am concerned that someone has been on my property. After a little investigation, I realized that I never closed it all the way.

As a Bronxonian, born and raised in the Bronx, New York, and who knows the unwritten code of the neighborhood, "Don't leave your door unlocked or unguarded," I am always watchful for unlocked doors, windows, or open gates on my property. The reason I installed locks on the doors and gates around my property is that I don't want any surprises from uninvited visitors. I live by a principle that says "What you build, you must protect; [if not] you will suffer the pain of discipline or the pain of regret." We spend a lot of time and energy trying to achieve a level of success. We spend thousands of dollars on education and hours upon hours during the week to earn an income. We then use our earnings to purchase property, but to not protect that property is a waste of our time and effort.

One day, while I was working in the yard with the gate open, a big stray dog came through the gate. I had to maneuver my way out of the yard and lock the gate behind me until the owner arrived and was able to secure his dog. This experience was yet, another reminder of not only why I put the gate up in the first place, but also why I needed to guard it and everything that it protects. This reminded me of how vulnerable we can become when our gates are not guarded. I was fortunate that this was a big fun loving dog, but what if it was a rabid dog? That's why you have to *Guard Your Gates!*

PERSONAL REFLECTIONS

THE GUARD YOUR GATES SYSTEM

ORGANIZE

DEFEND

GUARD

ROD PATTERSON

Guard Your Gates is my answer to managing incoming streams of information. It is a three step system that is easy to remember and simple to deploy.

The first step in the Guard Your Gates system is to **Organize**. In Jim Collins' book, "*Good to Great*", he uses a metaphor of a bus and driver to describe what a CEO should do to take his company to the next level. In his analogy, the company is symbolized as a bus and the CEO is represented by the driver of the bus. He explained that when a company is ready to go to the next level, they have to have the right people in placed to guide the company along. They have to assess which individuals are committed to moving the company forward and which ones are just going along for the ride. This is before they make decisions on what actions to take to move the company to the next level. In other words, the company has to get organized first. The company must decide who is on their "bus" and make sure the right people are in the right seats before the driver puts the bus into drive.

The late, Stephen Covey, author of the best-selling book, *The 7 Habits of Highly Effective People*, provides incredible insight in "Putting First Things First". It is in the spirit of Mr. Covey's third of his seven habits that our first step is derived. The third habit is the habit of personal responsibility. It helps you prioritize so what is most important is not at the mercy of what is least important. In the Guard Your Gates system, to organize means to understand the challenge, the obstacle, or the issue you are facing and prioritize accordingly.

"Give me six hours to chop down a tree and I

will spend the first four sharpening the axe." - Abraham Lincoln

Preparation is the key to making real progress. By making organization a primary objective, you save yourself so much time in accomplishing a task. Sometimes we think that we just need to dive in. We see a challenge, and then off we go to tackle it. We check our email inbox and see that it is flooded with new emails, and then off we go to responding to them one by one. We check our voicemail at work and notice that it has numerous messages and off we go to returning them one by one. The Nike coporation launched a successful advertising campaign coined, "Just Do It" in the late 1980s. It spoke to the need to take action. It spoke against procrastination. It was over-the-top popular. That is often the slogan that comes to mind when people just dive in and do not organize before tackling a problem.

The Guard Your Gates system does not say "Just Do It." You cannot "Just Do It". You can "Do It" effectively if you plan first. A task can seem so daunting when you look at it as a whole. However, when you break it down into bite-sized pieces, you will find it quite doable.

Take it from a parent. I am confident my experience is echoed among countless parents all over the country. At some point I decided to volunteer my services to my woeful teenagers and help them clean their rooms. I go into their room and there before me is the site of an obvious tornado with everything strewn all over the room. Dirty clothes and clean clothes mixed together dancing on the floor. Forks and plates we had been looking for months ago lay on the floor begging to be rescued. In short, I regret my decision and decided to back out. LOL! Then, I took a breath and started to organize. Once I began to size up the job and set some goals and outline my attack strategy, I began to see that it was not as terrible as I thought.

Getting organized is critical in the Guard Your Gates system because if you "Just Do It", you may get the wrong things done first and not necessarily make progress.

The next step in the Guard Your Gates system is to **Defend**. I am reminded of an ancient story of a leader who was determined to save his home town. He was living elsewhere when he got word that his town was in shambles. When he arrived, he found that the gates that kept the town protected were burned down. With the gates down, his people were vulnerable and defenseless. The leader was distressed about the condition of his people and was determined to help. Whether he knew it or not, this leader was obviously familiar with the Guard Your Gates system because the first thing he did was organize. He first organized the other leaders in the town and together they strategized how to protect the city and rebuild the gates. The town rallied and began to implement the strategy laid out by the leaders. The only problem was that when the neighboring people saw the work beginning and the gates to the city being rebuilt, they started trying to intimidate and bully the leaders into abandoning their efforts to rebuild. This is where the second step in the Guard You Gates system kicked in. The leader instructed the builders of the wall, to work with their tool in one hand but to hold a weapon in the other.

They needed to be ready to defend what they were building. In other words, while you are continuing to complete your task, be ready to fend off any distractions.

Defending your position is critical. My pastor once said that "Life is a fight for territory. When you stop fighting for what you want, what you don't want will step in and take over the territory." When you don't defend the gains that you've made in your career or the gains that you've made in your life, then those gains can easily be lost. The Guard Your Gates system includes defending because we don't want to experience leakage. In a business, leakage can occur when a business is succeeding and earning income on the frontend, but on the backend the company is experiencing a lot of waste in unnecessary expenses. Perhaps the resources are not being adequately managed and overspending is occurring. The gates of the company's success are not being defended or insulated against the leakage of unnecessary expenses. While advances are being made, the gates of the company's success are not being defended.

The Guard Your Gates system's "**Defend**" strategy is comparable to what happens on a football field every Sunday during the NFL season.

Imagine your team is on defense. You made some gains but now you are trying to keep those gains. Your opponent is on offense. Their goal is to steal ground from you. There is a line of demarcation that separates you from your opponent. The defensive line's job is to hold their ground and to keep the other team from moving past that line of demarcation. This is what it is like in the Guard Your Gates system. We have to defend our line of success from things like distractions or crisis that may cause a leak and take away from that success. We defend our line. If by chance we experience any leakage, we keep the situation from getting worse. It's like triaging a crisis. It's like stopping the bleeding. We must defend as we build and gain success.

Recall our story, the leader told the men building the wall to defend the work they were accomplishing. In so doing, the men were able to finish rebuilding the wall in record time.

The third step in the Guard Your Gates system is to **Guard**. Some may wonder what the difference between Guarding and Defending is. Guarding is taking preventative measures, while Defending is your response to an attack. A person fighting a disease will take medication to fend off the attack of the disease. However, a person guarding their health will exercise and avoid unhealthy foods to reduce the risk of getting sick. When we Guard, we place a boarder around our victories. When we fail to guard, that is when we come under attack and lose ground.

How many of us go through life in "La La Land?" We allow information to drift in and out of our lives without scrutiny. We are often so good at what we do that we don't take time to assess and evaluate whether or not we are actually progressing. Movement is not necessarily progress. Just because we are moving, it does not mean we are progressing.

Recently, I began to notice and uptick in my email inbox. I had started getting new emails concerning people I knew about updates on their social media pages. Some of it was interesting, but, at some point, I found myself not reading them at all. Then a brilliant idea came to me: Why not change my notifications settings on this social media site that was generating so many emails? My guards were down. Because I did not guard my email inbox, I now had to organize and defend my email. Does this make sense?

Guards are necessary to protect what is valuable. We have all heard of teenagers with fake identification cards who try to sneak into clubs so they can mingle with adults. That action is a threat to the owners of the club who have invested heavily in building and designing a respectable club for mature adults. They complied with all kinds of governmental regulations to open the club. In order to continue to protect their investment, they hire "guards" to protect the club, not only from the possibility of serving drinks to a minor, but also from individuals acting in an unruly manor. The guards protect the integrity of the club by keeping minors out and the club's environment by keeping the peace.

Likewise, the "Guard" step in the Guard Your Gates system is designed to protect what you consider valuable. After you have organized and defended that which is important to you, now it is time to guard it. When your gates are adequately guarded, you are able to quickly organize and defend against any threats. When your guards are up, you are ready to face an potential problems and may deflect matters before they become a "problem."

PERSONAL REFLECTIONS

_____

_____

_____

_____

_____

_____

_____

_____

_____

_____

ROD PATTERSON

EMAIL GATE

ROD PATTERSON

Do you carry an overwhelming number of unread emails in your inbox? Do you find co-workers complaining that you never read your emails? Have you ever lied about reading an email or by saying you never received it to avoid being embarrassed? If so, you are not alone.   You receive so many emails in an hour that it is often hard to keep up with.

One day my daughter caught a glimpse of my personal email inbox and exclaimed, "3000 unread emails?!" Her eyes were opened wide because she was clearly shocked.   She could not believe that I had that many emails that I had not opened. The truth is that her remark made me a little uncomfortable and embarrassed.

At home, I expend a lot of energy trying to maintain and organize our living space. Because I value neatness and structure, my daughter's comment made me look like a hypocrite. I immediately began to unsubscribe to websites that had been flooding my inbox with multiple emails. Her comment made sense! Why should I have that many unread emails in my inbox? It was time to **Organize**, **Defend**, and **Guard** my email gate.

Our email gates are very active and filled with critical information. They are also cluttered with information that is totally unrelated to the work we do. Sometimes we may have emails in our inbox that don't even belong to us because they were sent to us in error. What ends up happening is that critical emails that need our attention get buried in volumes of unrelated, unimportant, or unintended emails in our inbox. Have you ever scrolled through your email and found one from someone that you should have responded to by now? It is embarrassing and can affect how you are viewed.

Your email also contains many distractions. Not that their email is not important, or that you do not welcome or appreciate it, but in the moment, it diverts your focus from where it needs to be. It may include an email from a friend or loved one that distracts you from other priorities. It can also include emails from marketers fishing for clients that you unknowingly subscribed to. How do you filter your email so that you do not miss the most important ones? When this gate is not managed well, critical communications fall through the cracks. This gate must be managed to avoid the consequences of missing deadlines and to optimize your productivity. Take a look at your email inbox. How many unread emails do you have? Is it time for you to **Organize**, **Defend**, and **Guard**? Here are some basics that I encourage you to consider:

ORGANIZE

Here's how you do it:

- Flag important emails that you need to

respond to. Do this even if you are unable to respond to the emails right away.

- Sort your emails according to topic or sender

- Delete marketing emails that you do not intend to pursue

- Create folders for emails you want to refer back to later.

- File important emails in subfolders. Do this especially with emails that pertain to a specific project or event.

DEFEND

Here's how you do it:

- Unsubscribe to marketing emails you are no

longer interested in. These emails come daily or even multiple times throughout the day which only clutter your inbox giving you more emails to sift through to get to important ones.

• Unsubscribe to journals, newsletters, and trade magazines that you no longer read. Even if you are still interested in the publication, if you haven't gotten around to reading them in the last six months, unsubscribe. This will reduce the number of emails that make it to your inbox.

• Use your personal email address for correspondence unrelated to work.

GUARD

Here's how you do it:

•   Check your email regularly. Do not let days or even hours go by without checking your email. If you fail to check them regularly, you will allow your emails to accumulate and get to an unmanageable level. When this happens, it can affect your motivation to even read them at all.

•   Use auto filing macros to automatically flag and store emails by category. Let me explain. You can set macros to automatically color code emails you receive from specific people, like your manager, colleagues, or certain clients. The macros can even automatically place these emails in a specific folder so you can review them later. At the same time, it removes them from the email pool so they will not get lost.

Email is one of the primary ways professionals communicate. Quite often very important correspondence is sent via email that requires either a prompt response or includes a deadline. If the deadline is missed because of an overwhelmed email inbox, sometimes it can cost you your job. Don't get caught unprepared. Boost your productivity by guarding your email gate.

PERSONAL REFLECTIONS

_____

_____

_____

_____

_____

_____

_____

_____

_____

_____

_____

ROD PATTERSON

MOBILE PHONE GATE

ROD PATTERSON

What did we do before mobile phones were invented? It is nearly impossible these days to work effectively without a mobile phone. I have a Baby-Boomer friend who used to refuse to use a mobile phone. Even though he had one, he simply refused to use it. We were both volunteering for the same organization and were on the same team, so from time to time, I had to call him. It was so frustrating having to leave a message for him on his home phone. As a GenXer, I needed information now (LOL)! Eventually, he relented and started using his mobile phone.

I use my mobile phone all the time. It really

shouldn't be called a mobile phone. Think of all the things you can do with a smartphone. You can talk, text, take pictures, record videos, and so much more. It is actually a computer with phone-calling capabilities. My phone is rarely more than a few feet away from me at any given time, and maybe the same is true for you. So, with mobile phones being such a huge part of our lives, how should we manage them?

The truth is that mobile phones have changed our expectations when it comes to communication. Mobile phones have made communication easier. Just like I wanted instant answers from my friend, customers also want instant answers. They want answers now! (In the voice of Jack Bauer for those of you who watched "24") And, in most cases, there is no reason why they should not or cannot have them now. Put yourself in the customer's shoes. Have you ever tried to reach someone who had critical information for you to only get their voicemail? No matter how many times you called them, that's when you get their voicemail. Not only did they not answer your call, but they never even called you back. This can be extremely frustrating, especially, if there is a crisis happening, and the one person who can help does not answer their cell phone. How well you manage your mobile phone can impact how effective you are, because mobile phones have made communication a lot easier and much timelier.

Everyone manages their phones differently. Some of us refuse to answer our phones while we are in a meeting. Others never let their phones go to voice mail. And others would rather let calls go to voicemail and then return the calls later. There are many ways to manage your cell phone, but the point is, it's good to have a system.

So, if you have ever checked your voicemail to only hear: "Your voicemail is full," it is time to **Organize**, **Defend**, and **Guard** your mobile phone gate.

ORGANIZE

Here's how you do it:

•   Check your voicemail often

•   Prioritize your calls and return them all

•   Return calls as soon as possible, but within 24 hours

•   Delete voicemails once the call is returned

•   If you are unable to return the call immediately, write down the message in a place where you will not forget quickly and can easily retrieve it, but remember to return the call later, and delete the voicemail

DEFEND

Here's how you do it:

• Answer calls as they come in and avoid letting them go to voicemail

• Add special ringtones for your critical contacts (your spouse, children, manager, team members, etc.…)

• Leave details in your voicemail greeting about other ways to reach you, i.e., email and fax and how to send you information

• Update your greeting when you are taking personal time off from work, out of the office, or away from work on business and may not be able to return calls until you return

GUARD

Here's how you do it:

- Don't casually give out your mobile number you use for work to friends (and certain family members) -- LOL!

- Again, answer your phone

The key to managing your mobile phone gate is answering your phone. This saves you time. I do however, recognize that there are calls that you intentionally want to go to your voicemail. If you have friends or family members that like to call you during business hours that create a distraction for you, then yes, send them to voicemail. Those are the calls you want to pick up or return when you actually have adequate time available to actually talk to them. However, generally, when you answer your phone and avoid letting it go to voicemail, it

eliminates the need to return the call later. Be

known for being available and reliable. You can do

this by organizing, defending, and guarding your

mobile phone gate.

PERSONAL REFLECTIONS

_____

_____

_____

_____

_____

_____

_____

_____

_____

_____

ROD PATTERSON

OFFICE PHONE GATE

ROD PATTERSON

Have you ever returned from vacation and checked your office phone voicemail to hear the recording: "Your voicemail is full?" Yikes! It seems like people were waiting for you to leave your desk or take a day off to leave a message on your office phone. At least, with your mobile phone you have the opportunity to avoid a message by answering your phone, but with your office phone, you have no such luck. Why do we even need office phones these days, anyway? Well, your office looks incomplete without one. Also, landlines are critical when mobile signals are affected by weather, and who knows whatever else. The problem is that if you are out of the office, then your inbox on your office phone can become full.

In business and in life, communication is critical. Any unanswered call or unreturned message could mean a lost sale, lost account, or lost opportunity. Today's office phones have so many features that it can make missing calls a thing of the past. Some of the cool features include:

- Special ring tones for important stakeholders
- A built-in directory so you don't have to search frantically for your manager's, or other key colleagues phone numbers
- In case you receive messages that should be handled by someone else, a call forwarding feature that can save you the time of taking a message and

tracking down the person it belongs to.

Learning how to use these features is essential to managing your office phone. If I am in my office when a call comes in, I will pick up my phone. Even if someone is in my office, I will ask them to excuse me, and still pick it up and take a message or respond. I do this even at the risk of being accused of not giving my undivided attention to the person in my office. Unless I am in a crucial state in the face-to-face conversation, I will answer the phone. Why? It saves me time. It also boosts my image, my personal brand of being available and responsive. While I do believe there are times when you should let your phone calls go to voicemail, in most cases you can answer the call and get back to your conversation. Most conversations at the office are rarely free of interruptions, anyway. So, while I value uninterrupted conversations, it is also important to **Organize**, **Defend** and **Guard** my office phone.

ORGANIZE

Here's how you do it:

- Clear your voicemail often
- Prioritize your calls and return them all
- Update your voicemail when you are not in the office or when you are going to be away from your desk for an extended period of time (2 hours or more)

DEFEND

Here's how you do it:

- Answer your phone and avoid letting it go to voicemail

- Add special ringtones to your critical contacts

GUARD

Here's how you do it:

- Answer your phone

- Don't casually give out your office phone number to friends (and certain family members)

- Leave a meaningful and detailed greeting, especially when you are going to be out of the office

• Forward your office phone to your mobile phone when you are working remotely. This will minimize the need to check your office voicemail too often. However, you should still check your office voicemail throughout the day for the calls that may not have forwarded to your mobile phone.

For those of us who, at times, work remotely, but also maintain an office, guarding your desk phone can be a challenge. Even if you have a Secretary, Administrative Assistant, Executive Assistant, or someone who can pick up messages for you, you still need to check in for those messages. If your desk phone has features that can help you route calls to your mobile phone, use it.

That is an important tool in guarding your desk

phone.

PERSONAL REFLECTIONS

_____

_____

_____

_____

_____

_____

_____

_____

_____

_____

_____

TASK GATE

ROD PATTERSON

My wife is the master at giving herself reminders. Her phone buzzes constantly to remind her of "this and that." She is really amazing. I, on the other hand, used to trust my brain to help me remember everything. Well, I have now adopted her method. Why? Because it is impossible to remember all the things that I need to keep up with. Eventually, something important is going to get missed. Usually what are missed are not the trivial matters. It is something that will throw you into crisis mode.

What is a task? It is something that you need to get done by a specific date and/or time. I have so many tasks to complete that I sometimes get tired of setting reminders! Honestly speaking, this is not my strongest suit. Managing tasks has always been a challenge for me.

I remember being in a meeting with senior management, and one of them asked if a task--not extremely important task--but still important--was done. I honestly could not recall, but when I checked, I was relieved that I had done it.

As a leader, I sometimes assign tasks to my team, obviously, to accomplish them and I can tell you it is such a pleasure and comfort to know that the task I assigned was completed. However, it is annoying and disappointing to discover that a delegated task is still outstanding.

In managing your tasks, it is best to have a system. I primarily use a notebook to organize my tasks. After I write down all of the things I have to do, I then prioritize them. Your tasks should not only include those daily items related to work, but they should also include items related to your goals because your overall success is tied to your daily accomplishments. So now, it is time to **Organize**, **Defend**, and **Guard** task gate.

ORGANIZE

Here's how you do it:

- Check your tasks daily and often

- Sort your tasks according to priority

- Tasks from management should always be given top priority

- Remember to delete completed tasks so they do not clog your calendar

DEFEND

Here's how you do it:

- If your tasks are overwhelmed and overwhelming, sort them by priority and then do the critical ones first

GUARD

Here's how you do it:

- Check your tasks regularly

- Delegate tasks to others, if possible

- Schedule your tasks with intentionality

- Do not schedule more tasks than you can realistically get to in any given day

Some people manage their tasks by making a list. Others use sticky notes on their computer monitor. And still, others may use their smart phones or computer systems to remind them of the things on their "to-do" list.

When it comes to technology, I am reminded of a story shared by Stephen Covey in his book *First Things First*. He told the story of a very wealthy man who wanted a beautiful garden. The man wanted everything done automatically. He

called the top technologically-advanced gardener he

could find. He told the gardener he wanted:

Automatic sprinkling systems

Automatic weed remover

Automatic feeding system

Automatic lawn mowing

Automatic trimming

The gardener stopped writing and stared and

the millionaire and the millionaire said, "What's

wrong?" The gardener replied, "I understand that

you want everything done automatically, but realize

this: No gardener, no garden!"

The gardener's reply with regards to your

tasks and using technology is so true. While technology is good, you must still manage your tasks, and you must do it proactively.

Whatever the method, the key is to organize these tasks into manageable groups. I heard someone say the only way to eat an elephant is to eat it one bite at a time. The same applies to your tasks. One task at a time! This will help you guard your task gate well.

PERSONAL REFLECTIONS

CALENDAR GATE

ROD PATTERSON

Do you control your own calendar? At some companies, a manager or an assistant may have the ability to place events on your calendar. I have always been a hawk about my calendar and email. I watch over my calendar to ensure that it does not only include what others have on their agenda for me but that it also includes what I have on my agenda for me, plans and ideas for my growth. It includes goals and aspirations of my own. When your calendar is overrun with events, it is time to **Organize**, **Defend** and **Guard**.

Here are some things that should definitely be on your calendar, but not necessarily in this order:

- Mentor/Mentee meetings

- Relationship building with key clients

- Necessary meetings

- Family Time

I heard that the only target you will hit is the one you aim at. Do you set goals? Do you set timeframes for accomplishing them? Your progress should be measurable. When you don't set goals for yourself, others will make you a part of achieving their goals. Be proactive about setting goals for your growth and development, your own ideas and aspirations.

Spending time with your mentor or mentee

is important. Your mentor is the person that is guiding you to help you accomplish your goals. Your mentee is the one you are guiding. It is your "thank you" for all of the help you received from your mentor. You "pay it forward" by mentoring someone else. Your mentor is probably busy filling up their calendar, so be intentional about getting on it. At the same time, reserve calendar space for time with your mentee.

When you fail to guard your calendar gate, there will be no room on your calendar for this key meeting with your mentor or mentee.

Do you spend time with your key clients?

Building lasting relationships require time. Be intentional about regularly carving out time in your calendar for your key relationships. When you do this, your clients feel important. I have one vendor that I use who regularly checks in to see how things are going. So guess what? I think of that vendor first when I need services they can provide. When you guard your calendar gate this way, to ensure that it includes time for staying connected with key clients, it is easy to resolve problems when they arise. When a problem arises and you receive a call from your clients, they don't feel like strangers disrupting your day.

In the business world, family-time

sometimes get sacrificed. When you invest time with your family by including them on your calendar, they feel valued and are more understanding when you have to work late or go away on business. Don't neglect your family. Success everywhere else and failure at home is still failure.

Finally, if there is one thing I hate, it is unproductive meetings. Unnecessary meetings are even worse. Avoid them as much as you can!

So here's what I suggest if you want to guard your calendar gate:

ORGANIZE

Here's how you do it:

- Start by asking yourself a few questions like:

    o Can this meeting happen without me?

    o Am I adequately prepared for this meeting?

    o If the event or meeting is going to happen, then what is the agenda?

- Set goals

- Schedule time with your mentor/mentee

- Block out family time

DEFEND

Here's how you do it:

- Cancel the entire meeting if you are the host or decline your attendance if your presence is not required

- Block out free time on your calendar to strategize and plan moves and advancements in your career

- Schedule vacation

- Schedule time with your mentor and/or mentee in advance

GUARD

Here's how you do it:

- Check your calendar often

- Reply to invitations that will be added to your calendar if you accept them
- Say no or send a representative to meetings that don't require your personal attendance

The events and items that fill your calendar say a lot about what you value. If you say that you value continued education but your calendar is void of any training classes, you should ask yourself whether or not you truly value continued education. The same can be said about family time and socializing. If you say you love spending time with your family but they are nowhere on your calendar, then is that really true? It can still be true, but when you don't' add your values to your calendar, you run the risk of missing out on special time with your

family and friends and leaving your calendar gate

unorganized, undefended, and unguarded.

PERSONAL REFLECTIONS

DESK GATE

ROD PATTERSON

Have you ever walked into an office of a professional seeking their expertise on a matter and the condition of their desk caused you to question their ability to help you solve your problem?   I remember the first year or two of my marriage, my wife and I decided to use a family member to prepare our tax return. The family member was not the most organized, and I recall feeling uneasy about it. Her desk was a mess!   Needless to say, we were audited by the IRS the following year. We paid the penalty to the IRS but came away with a good analogy for my book.

Take a look at your desk right now. It

doesn't matter if you are at home or the office. If there is paperwork on your desk that you cannot identify, then you could have a time bomb buried there waiting to explode. When I go into the office of any of the company's executives, their desks are usually clear of paperwork. I am sure they receive just as much mail as anyone else. Admittedly, they may have an assistant to filter what actually makes it on to their desk, but you can do the same. If you do not have someone to filter through your mail for you, filter through it yourself and identify and decide what should find a place on your desk and what should not.

The truth is that we receive a lot of mail.

Whether it is from vendors looking for new business or bills sent by creditors, paperwork can pile up on your desk quickly. A cluttered look can give the appearance or be an indication that you are overwhelmed, and when you are overwhelmed, it is difficult to make good decisions. Because you sat on something too long that was buried under a pile on your desk, the decisions you make may be made under the pressure to get an answer out. Absent the pressure to get an answer out, you would have given a well thought out reply. However, now, your knee-jerk answer may have a worse effect than not replying at all. If this describes you in any way, just know that you can turn this thing around. It is time to **Organize**, **Defend**, and **Guard** your desk gate.

ORGANIZE

Here's how you do it:

• Have all mail scanned after you have reviewed it or scan it yourself if you don't have an assistant

• Acknowledge all correspondence received and then file away the document

• Use the "Touch it once" strategy. That means if you touch a piece of paper on your desk, do something with it right then and then file it away. It is amazing how quickly your desk will clear up!

•   Spend time organizing your file cabinets.
This will save you time later and help you easily put
away paperwork and find it when needed. (Another
strategy is to sort first and then apply the "Touch it
once" strategy.)

DEFEND

Here's how you do it:

•   Immediately return mail placed on your desk
in error to its rightful owner.

•   Ask your colleagues to check whether they
have any mail for you on their desk. Do this
especially if you were expecting to receive

correspondence that should have arrived already.

GUARD

Here's how you do it:

• Arrange for all your desk mail to be scanned when you know you are going to be out of the office and have them sent to you electronically.

I am probably a bit anal when it comes to my desk gate. Somehow, it takes on a more philosophical meaning. When I see my desk, whether at home or at work, cluttered with paperwork or mail or miscellaneous items, I ask myself "what does this mean?" Is my life like this?

Is my life this cluttered and disorganized? Those questions force me to immediately **Organize**, **Defend**, and then **Guard** my desk gate.

Whether it is coworkers dropping mail on your desk that does not belong to you or your child's class project piled up on your desk, be prepared to guard it.

PERSONAL REFLECTIONS

TIME GATE

ROD PATTERSON

The time gate is the most critical and is the most difficult gate to manage. This gate affects your ability to organize, defend, and guard all of your other gates. How do you manage your time? What happens when you do not effectively manage your time? You know what happens. Nothing good! Have you ever missed an important family event because you scheduled a critical meeting on the same day and at the same time? Usually, by the time you realize you made a mistake, it is too late to make an adjustment. Most likely, you are going to break someone's heart.

How do you define time management? What

tools do you use to help you manage your time? The reality is that you cannot manage time, but you can manage your life. Time management is life management!

The greatest enemy of time management is procrastination.

"Procrastination is a thief. It is defined as a symptom of some area of stress in your life. It is the avoidance of a task that needs to be accomplished." A. R. Bernard

Procrastination will rob you of valuable time and all that could have been accomplished with it.

118

Years ago, I learned a very hard lesson about procrastination. One of my brothers was very ill, in fact, in grave condition. One evening, I received an urgent call from my mother to come down to Philadelphia to see my brother, who was hospitalized and in the Intensive Care Unit. Instead of making the trip from New York to Philadelphia that night, I delayed my trip to the next day even though I had received an urgent call to be present. By the time I arrived, my brother had passed away a few hours before. My heart was broken, and it took me a long time to forgive myself for procrastinating my trip to Philadelphia. Needless to say, lesson learned. I rarely ever procrastinate, especially regarding matters that are urgent.

Perhaps you haven't had to pay as high a price as I have for procrastination, but if you have allowed this particular thief to steal opportunities and successes from you, then here is how you **Organize**, **Defend**, and **Guard** your time gate.

ORGANIZE

Here's how you do it:

• Outline what you are involved with. What are the different roles you have? Husband? Father? Manager? Leader?

• Clarify your values. Once your values are clear, then it will help you understand where to spend your time

DEFEND

Here's how you do it:

• Stop and make a judgment. Take and assessment of all that you are involved with and identify where you may be procrastinating. The best place to start is by looking at your goals. Also look at your tasks? Which goals have you accomplished? Which tasks are still outstanding? After you identify the areas that you are procrastinating in, make a firm decision to stop procrastinating and take action now! (Again, in my Jack Bauer voice for those of you who watched "24")

- Find an accountability partner. You need someone to hold you accountable for not procrastinating.

GUARD

Here's how you do it:

- Say no. Say it often. Don't let people steal time from you. Don't' be shy about saying "No" when you need to. Say it nicely and sincerely and without malice, but say "No." Realize that you simply cannot do everything and be everywhere and commit to every event.

- Do the most distasteful tasks first. People are prone to doing the tasks that bring them the most joy first. At the same time, it is easy to

procrastinate those tasks that you despise or feel are

beneath you. Therefore, instead of handling those

distasteful tasks, you use that time on the more

pleasurable, but less urgent, tasks.

Effectively guarding your time gate will

restore or give time back to you that would

otherwise be wasted. We all have seen or

experienced individuals who come over to our

desks unannounced and overstay their welcome.

All the while, the clock is ticking, and we are not

getting anything done. When this happens, you

have to be assertive in redirecting those people

away from your desk, of course you should do it

nicely, but you should and must do it nevertheless.

One of the most effective ways of guarding your time gate is by budgeting and allocating your time.   What do you spend time on? How much time you allow for Planning? Socializing? Resting? How much time do you allocate your for goal setting? When you don't budget your time, you can end up wondering, "Where did the time go?"

While the time gate is the most critical, it is probably the easiest to overlook. When it is managed effectively, however, you will be amazed at how much you get accomplished on any given day. At this point, I know I don't have to say it, but

I'll say it anyway: **Guard** your time gate!

PERSONAL REFLECTIONS

PULLING IT ALL TOGETHER

ROD PATTERSON

Recall my experience at the company I was with when I was affected by crisis? Crises are normal to life, and we all experience them at some point or another. What matters most is how we guard ourselves when a crisis occurs.

How do you Guard Your Gates when you are in crisis mode? The first step in securing your gates is being aware that you have gates that actually need to be guarded. So many of the activities we are involved with are done somewhat mechanically. We answer our phones, return emails, and respond to inquiries almost intuitively. That may work for a while, but when you do these things intentionally--with a plan--it can work well, even in your absence.

Take your email gate for example. If you experience a crisis that is going to take you out of the office for a while, make sure you leave a detailed message in your auto reply that will advise everyone that you are not available. It should also direct them to contact whoever is covering for you in your absence.

Take my example when HR called me in because they realized that I was being affected by my mother's illness. I should have taken a leave of absence at that point, longer than a week. Based on everything going on, one week was not enough time for me to regroup. If I had taken a short leave, then I would have been able to return to work strongly and continue my streak of success. Trying to manage a workload nonstop while in crisis mode, without taking adequate time to gain my bearings, was a recipe for failure. Perhaps, I could have reduced my work schedule as an alternative to taking a leave, but I should have been doing something to better guard my gates.

This is a message not only for employees, but employers as well. When HR called me in, perhaps they could have recommended that I take a short leave of absence to deal with my crisis, as opposed to granting me a one week reprieve. As an employee, I didn't want to seem inadequate. As an employer with greater insight and wisdom in dealing with employees in crisis, a recommendation to take an actual leave would have been welcomed. I am not putting the bulk of the responsibility on the employer, but if you have a valued employee, you may want to consider this approach. It costs employers thousands of dollars to recruit great talent. The old adage "It's cheaper to keep her!" may apply here.

Take the phone gates as a final example. During my crisis, I worked remotely a lot, so it was extremely challenging for me to keep up with my phone calls while on the road. I was managing three phones. I had two mobile phones, a personal one and one for business. I also had a desk phone in the office. That made three voicemails I had to check regularly. That affected my ability to respond to my customers and clients, not to mention family members calling to inquire about my mom's health. I was not successful in getting back to people timely, and in some cases, I did not get back to them at all.

Later in my career, when I reflected on how to better guard my mobile phone gate, I started using technology to have calls made to my office phone redirected to my office mobile phone. I also got rid of my personal mobile phone and did not give that number out any longer. That streamlined all of my calls to one gate when I was out of the office. When you do that, you will develop a reputation of regularly answering your phone, which translates into a reputation of reliability.

Guard Your Gates. A gate is just a pathway through which you receive information. When you don't guard those pathways, your gate, you will become vulnerable to attack. Your gate may not be listed above, but by now, you should know a gate when you see or experience one. Once you identify a gate, do whatever you have to do to **Organize**, **Defend**, and **Guard** your gate and watch your productivity explode!

134

GUARD YOUR GATES

ABOUT THE AUTHOR

Rod Patterson is a husband, father, and leader of men, public speaker, and blogger. He has worked in the insurance industry for more than 28 years and currently serves as an AVP Manager of Property claims. As an experienced public speaker, Rod speaks to hundreds of men in public presentations and through his blog, *The Lit Pathway,* teaching, mostly men, to become better versions of themselves.

Since 1997, Rod has volunteered for the International Christian Brotherhood (ICB) and currently serves as the ICB Coordinator responsible for leadership development, and brand expansion. ICB is a fraternity that gives men the tools needed to become leaders and valuable contributors to society.

Rod holds a B.S. in Marketing from York College and lives in Suffolk County on Long Island with his wife of over twenty five years, Katrina, and their two children Ericka and Shane.

ROD PATTERSON